GRAPHIC LIBRARY™

INVENTIONS AND DISCOVERY

ALEXANDER GRAHAM BELL AND THE
TELEPHONE

by Jennifer Fandel

illustrated by Keith Tucker

Consultant:
Michael E. Gorman
Professor of Science, Technology, and Society
University of Virginia
Charlottesville, Virginia

Capstone press®
Mankato, Minnesota

Graphic Library is published by Capstone Press,
151 Good Counsel Drive, P.O. Box 669, Mankato, Minnesota 56002.
www.capstonepress.com

Printed in the United States of America

1 2 3 4 5 6 11 10 09 08 07 06

Library of Congress Cataloging-in-Publication Data
Fandel, Jennifer.
Alexander Graham Bell and the telephone / by Jennifer Fandel; illustrated by Keith Tucker.
p. cm.— (Graphic library. Inventions and discovery)
Summary: "In graphic novel format, tells the story of how Alexander Graham Bell came up with the telephone, and how his invention changed the way people communicate"—Provided by publisher.
Includes bibliographical references and index.
ISBN-13: 978-0-7368-6478-7 (hardcover)
ISBN-10: 0-7368-6478-4 (hardcover)
ISBN-13: 978-0-7368-7513-4 (softcover pbk.)
ISBN-10: 0-7368-7513-1 (softcover pbk.)
1. Bell, Alexander Graham, 1847–1922—Juvenile literature. 2. Inventors—United States—Biography—Juvenile literature. 3. Telephone—History—Juvenile literature. I. Tucker, Keith. II. Title. III. Series.
TK6143.B4F36 2007
621.385092—dc22 2006004082

Designers
Jason Knudson and Kim Brown

Colorist
Sarah Trover

Editor
Christine Peterson

Editor's note: Direct quotations from primary sources are indicated by a yellow background.

Direct quotations appear on the following pages:
Pages 14–15, from the notebooks of Alexander Graham Bell; page 17, from a 1915 speech by Thomas Watson; page 20, from a letter written by Alexander Graham Bell to his father; part of the Alexander Graham Bell Family Papers at the Library of Congress (http:/memory.loc.gov/ammem/bellhtml/bellhome.html).
Pages 24 and 25, from Bell's account of the transcontinental phone call as published in *Alexander Graham Bell: The Life and Times of the Man Who Invented the Telephone* by Edwin S. Grosvenor and Morgan Wesson (New York: Harry Abrams, 1997).

TABLE OF CONTENTS

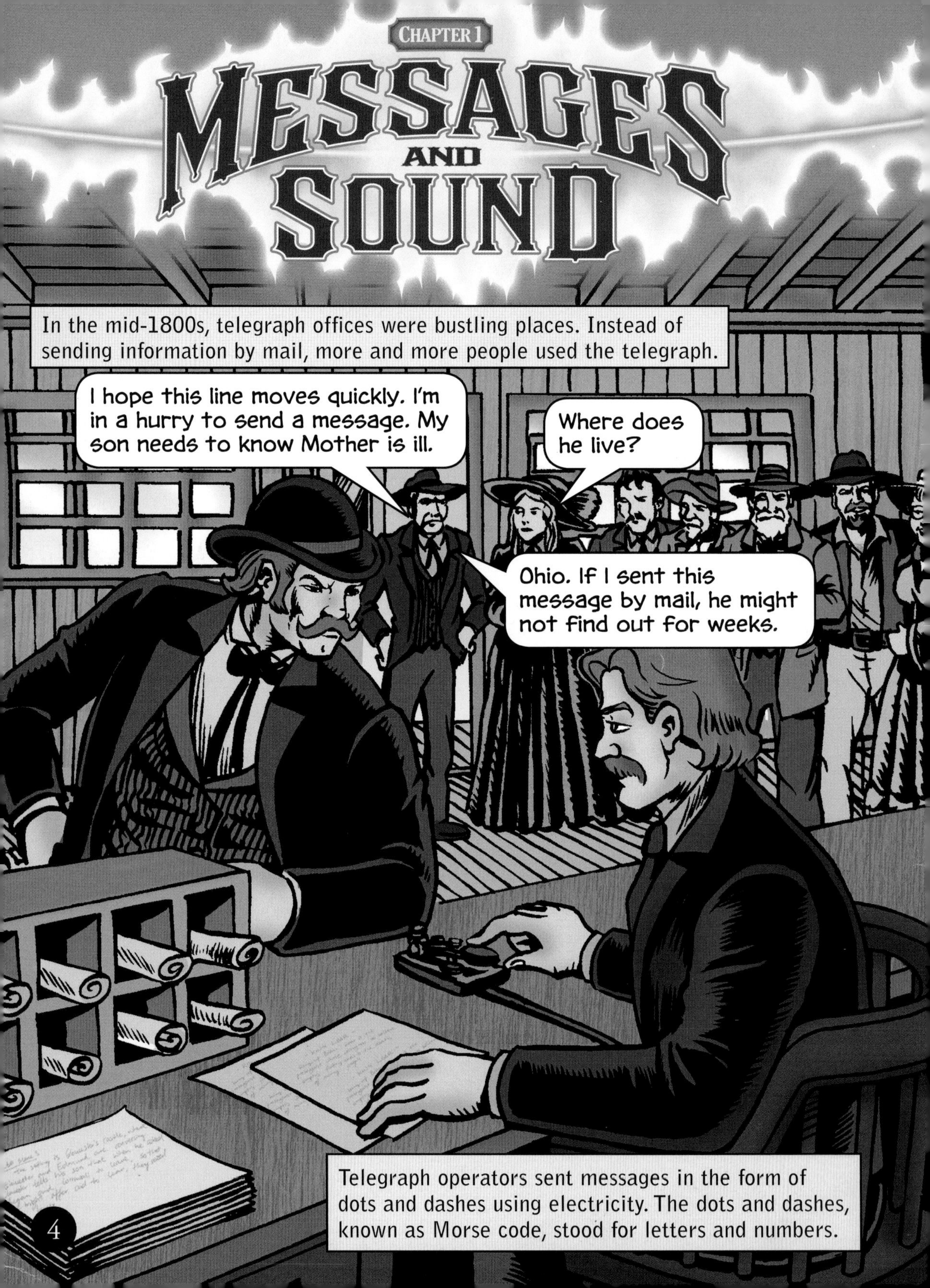
CHAPTER 1
MESSAGES AND SOUND
In the mid-1800s, telegraph offices were bustling places. Instead of sending information by mail, more and more people used the telegraph.
I hope this line moves quickly. I'm in a hurry to send a message. My son needs to know Mother is ill.
Where does he live?
Ohio. If I sent this message by mail, he might not find out for weeks.
Telegraph operators sent messages in the form of dots and dashes using electricity. The dots and dashes, known as Morse code, stood for letters and numbers.

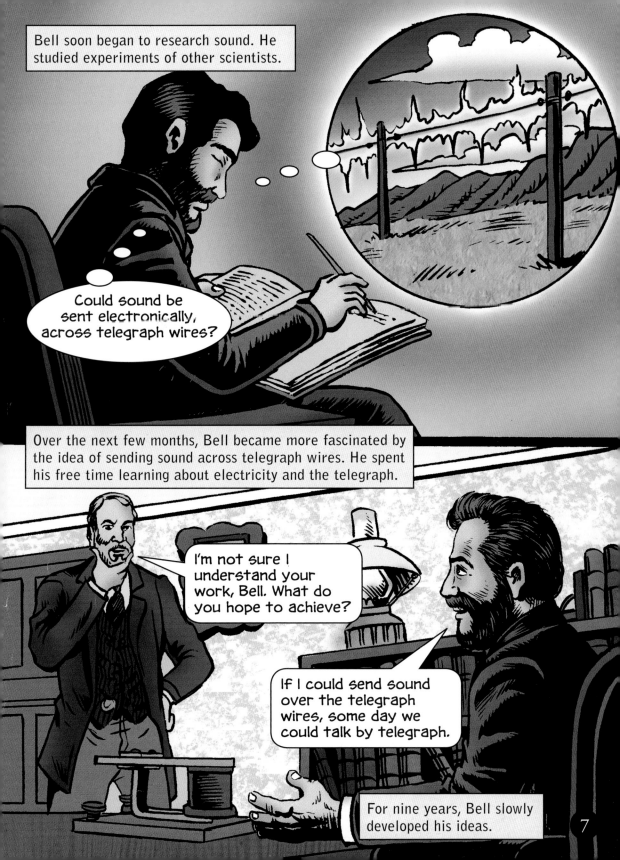

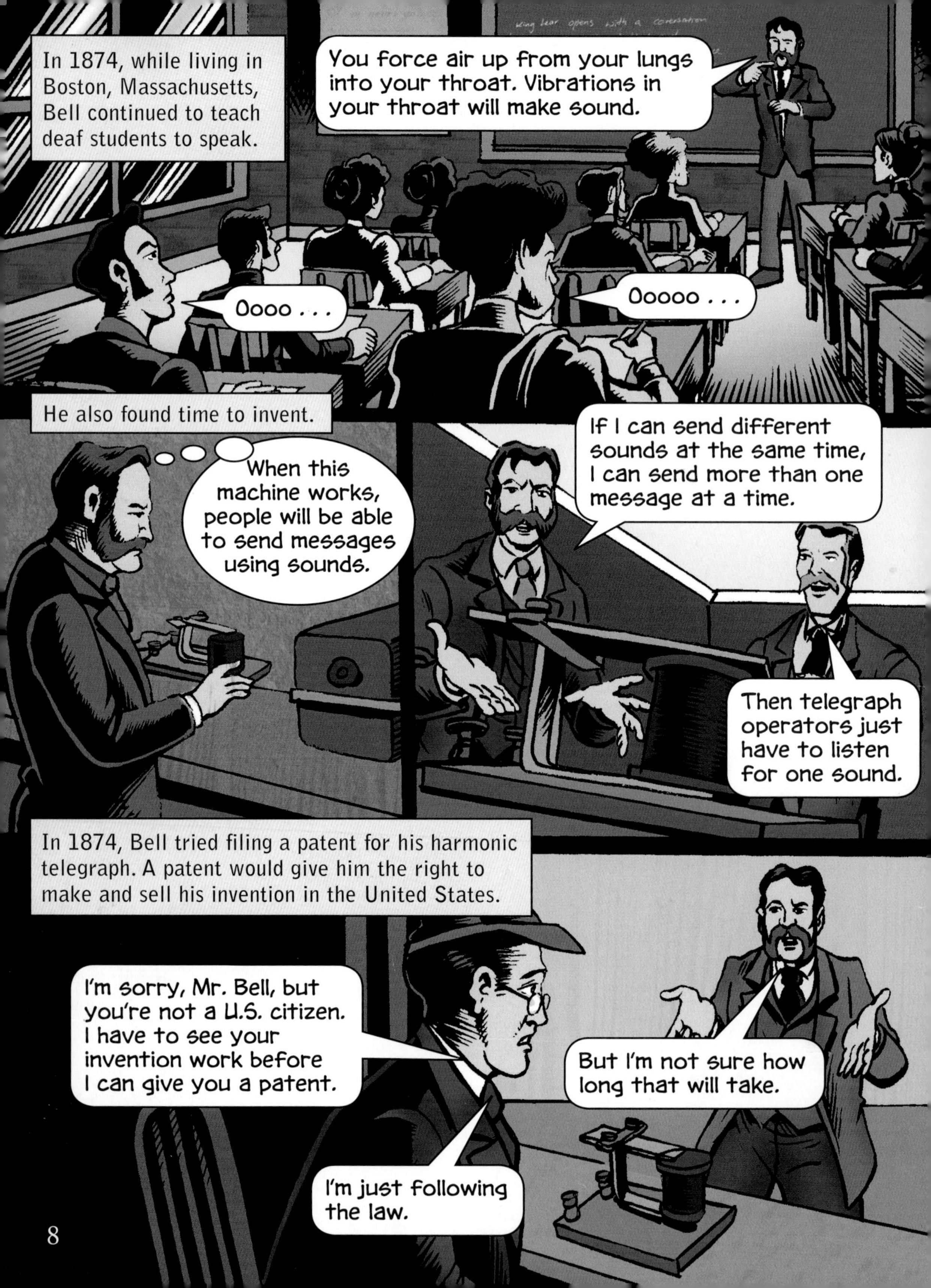
In 1874, while living in Boston, Massachusetts, Bell continued to teach deaf students to speak.
You force air up from your lungs into your throat. Vibrations in your throat will make sound.
Oooo . . .
Ooooo . . .
He also found time to invent.
When this machine works, people will be able to send messages using sounds.
If I can send different sounds at the same time, I can send more than one message at a time.
Then telegraph operators just have to listen for one sound.
In 1874, Bell tried filing a patent for his harmonic telegraph. A patent would give him the right to make and sell his invention in the United States.
I'm sorry, Mr. Bell, but you're not a U.S. citizen. I have to see your invention work before I can give you a patent.
But I'm not sure how long that will take.
I'm just following the law.

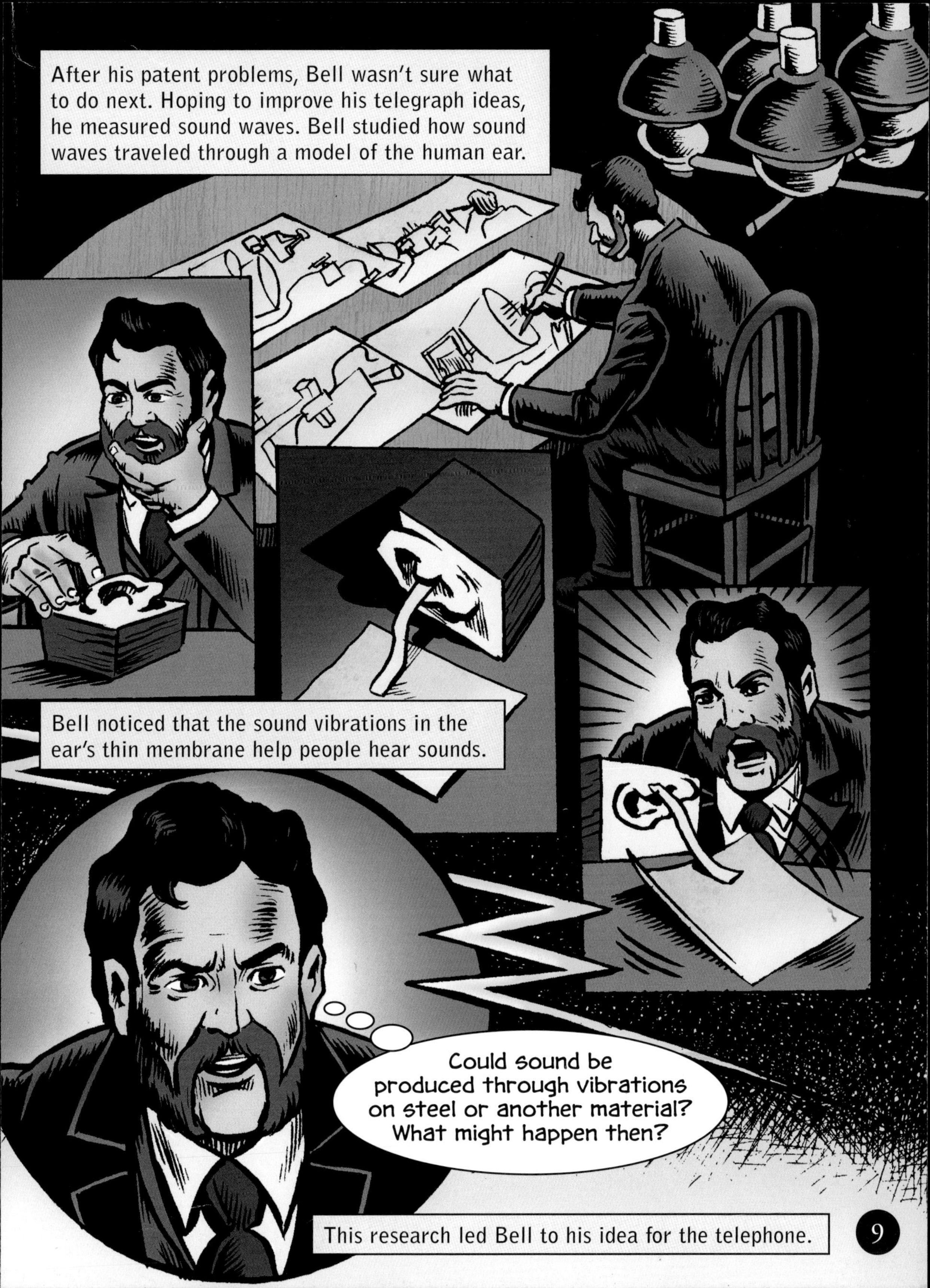
After his patent problems, Bell wasn't sure what to do next. Hoping to improve his telegraph ideas, he measured sound waves. Bell studied how sound waves traveled through a model of the human ear.
Bell noticed that the sound vibrations in the ear's thin membrane help people hear sounds.
Could sound be produced through vibrations on steel or another material? What might happen then?
This research led Bell to his idea for the telephone.

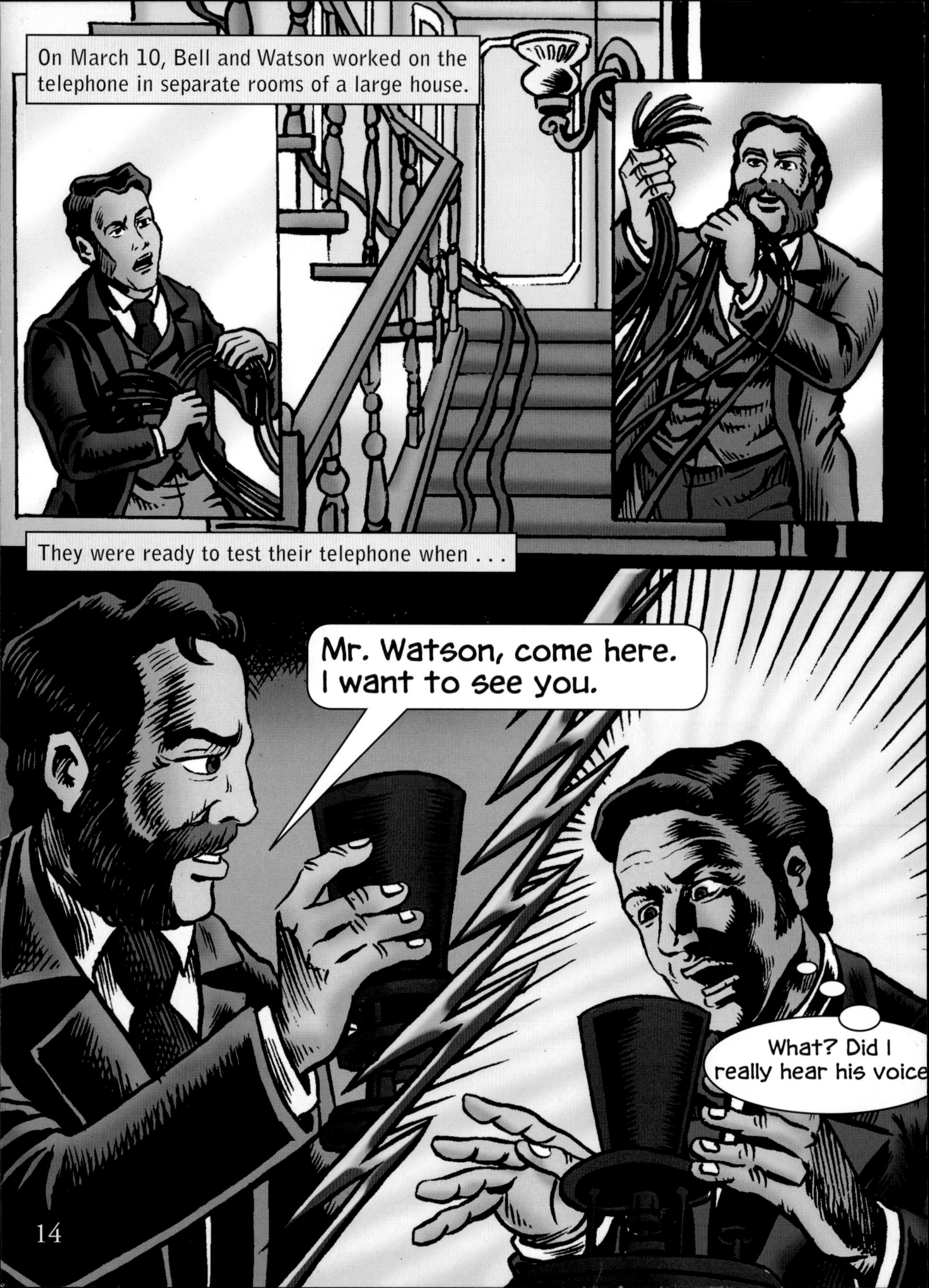
On March 10, Bell and Watson worked on the telephone in separate rooms of a large house.
They were ready to test their telephone when . . .
Mr. Watson, come here. I want to see you.
What? Did I really hear his voice

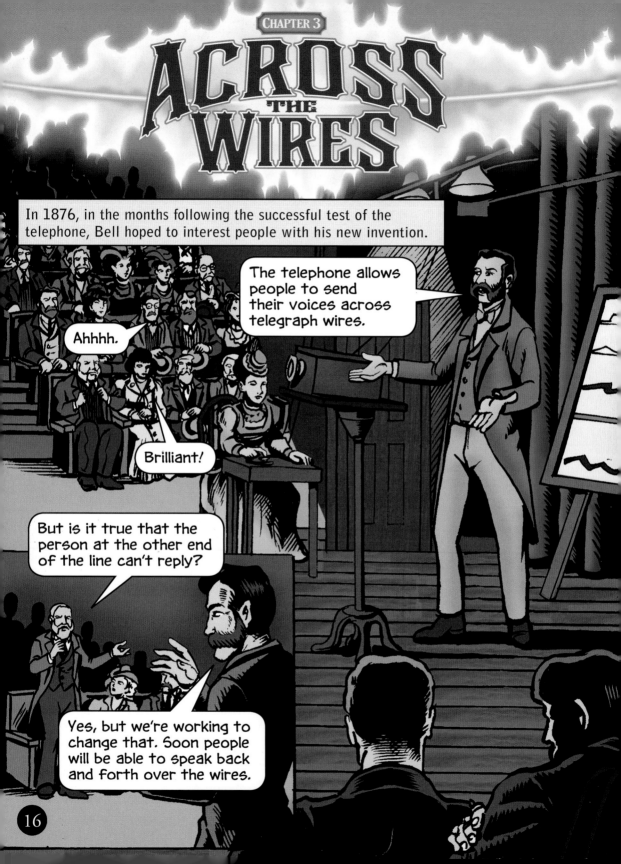

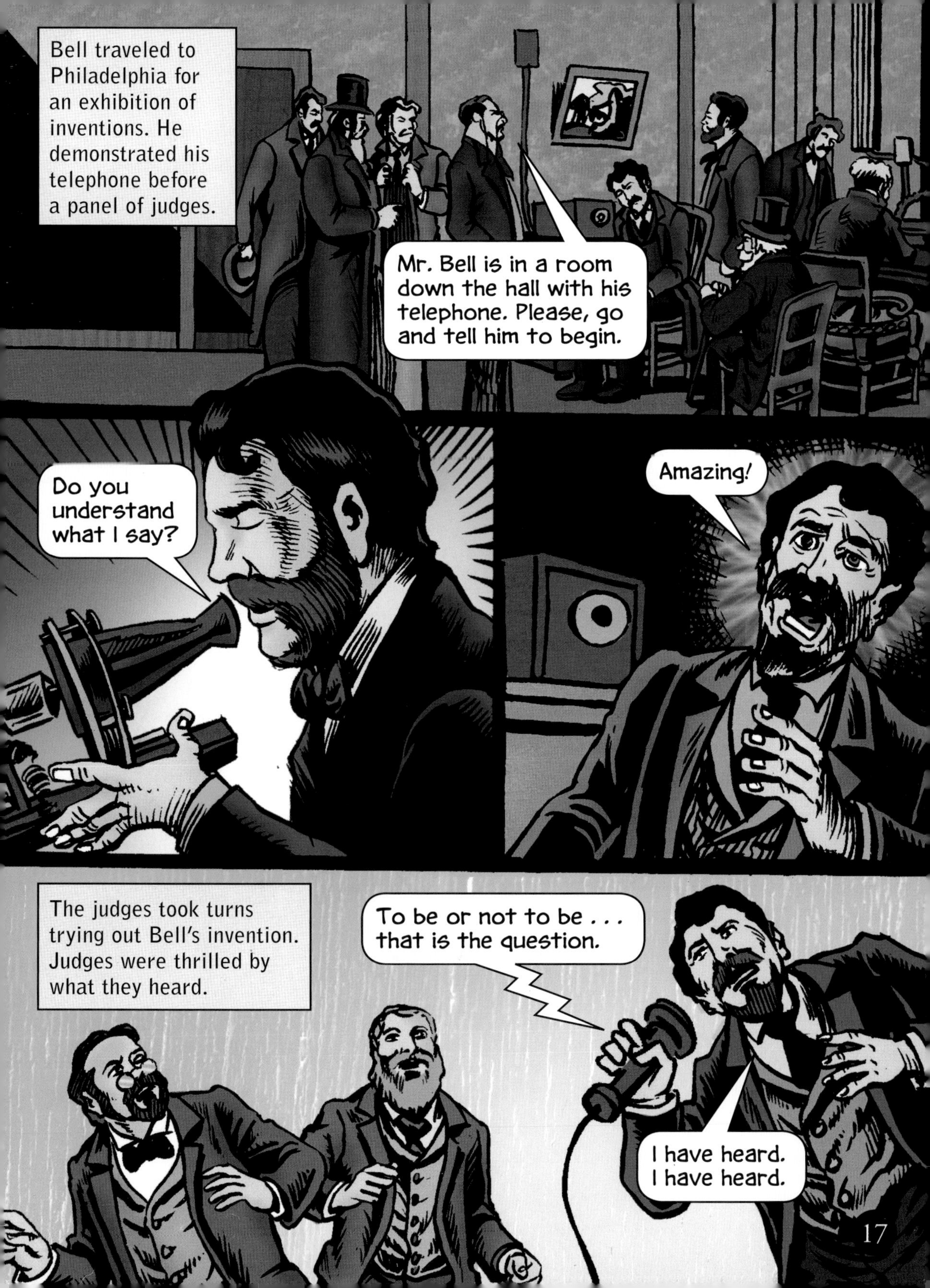
Bell traveled to Philadelphia for an exhibition of inventions. He demonstrated his telephone before a panel of judges.
Mr. Bell is in a room down the hall with his telephone. Please, go and tell him to begin.
Do you understand what I say?
Amazing!
The judges took turns trying out Bell's invention. Judges were thrilled by what they heard.
To be or not to be . . . that is the question.
I have heard. I have heard.

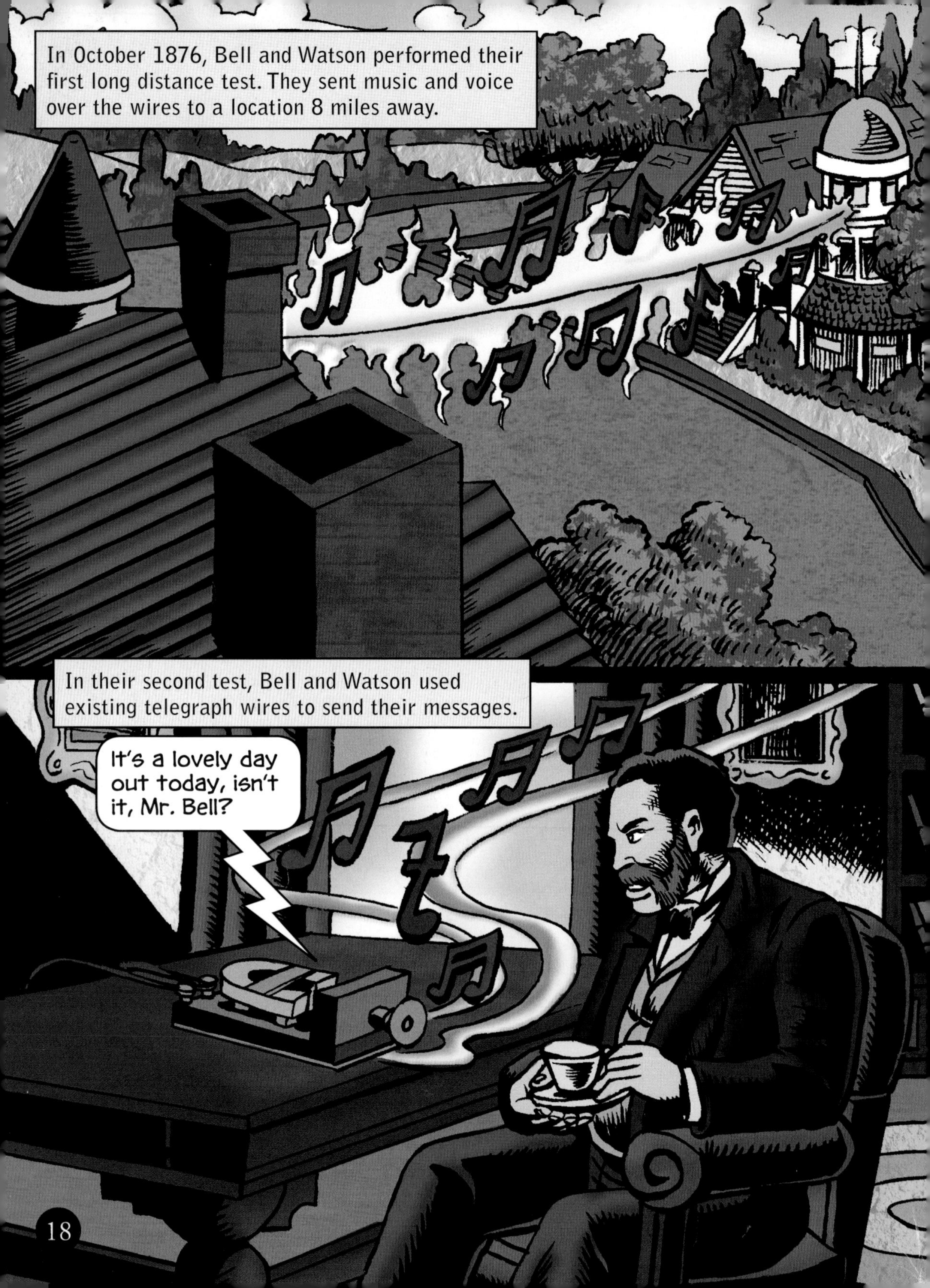
In October 1876, Bell and Watson performed their first long distance test. They sent music and voice over the wires to a location 8 miles away.
In their second test, Bell and Watson used existing telegraph wires to send their messages.
It's a lovely day out today, isn't it, Mr. Bell?

19

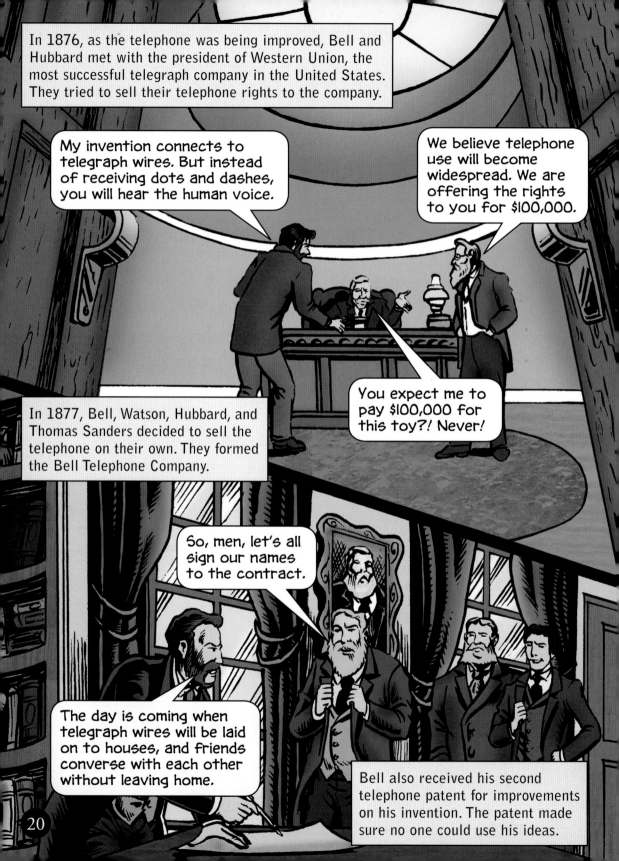

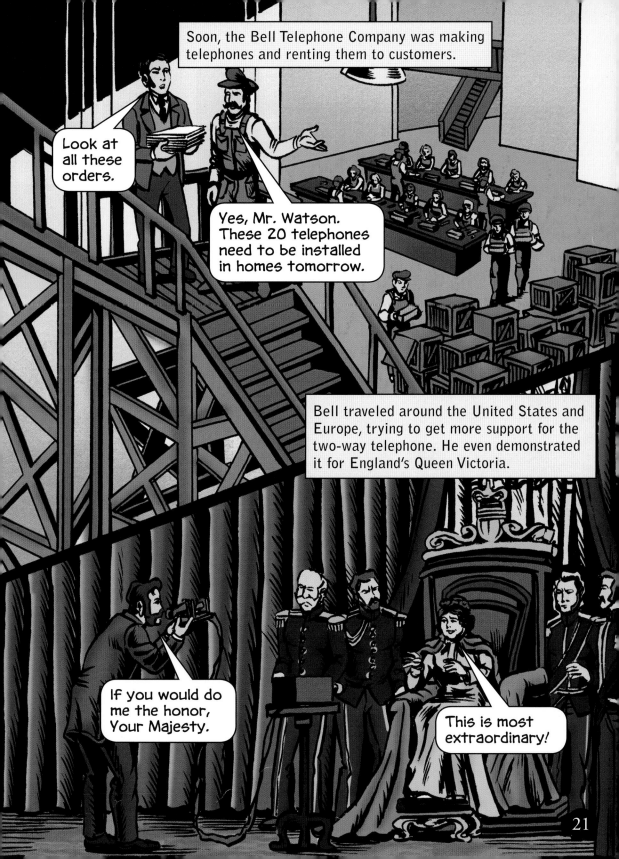

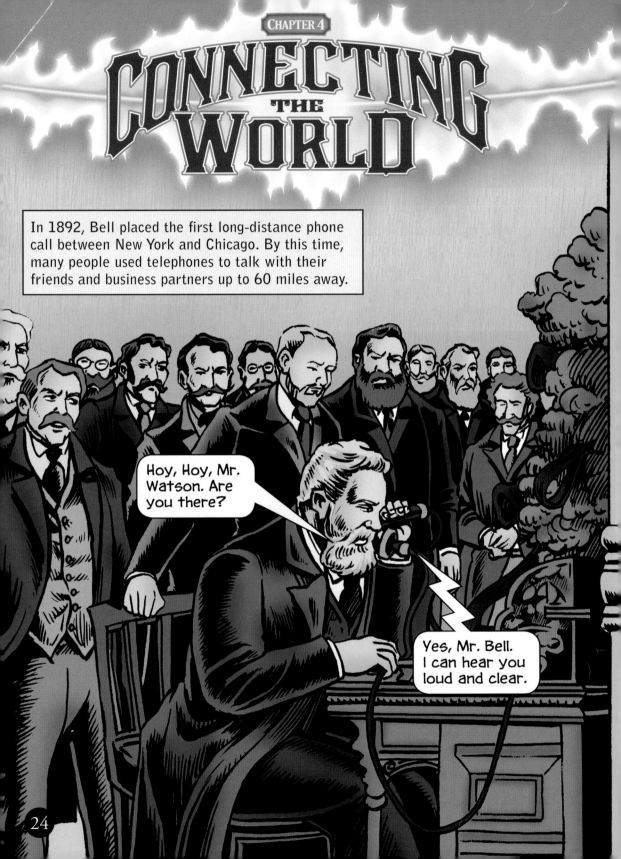

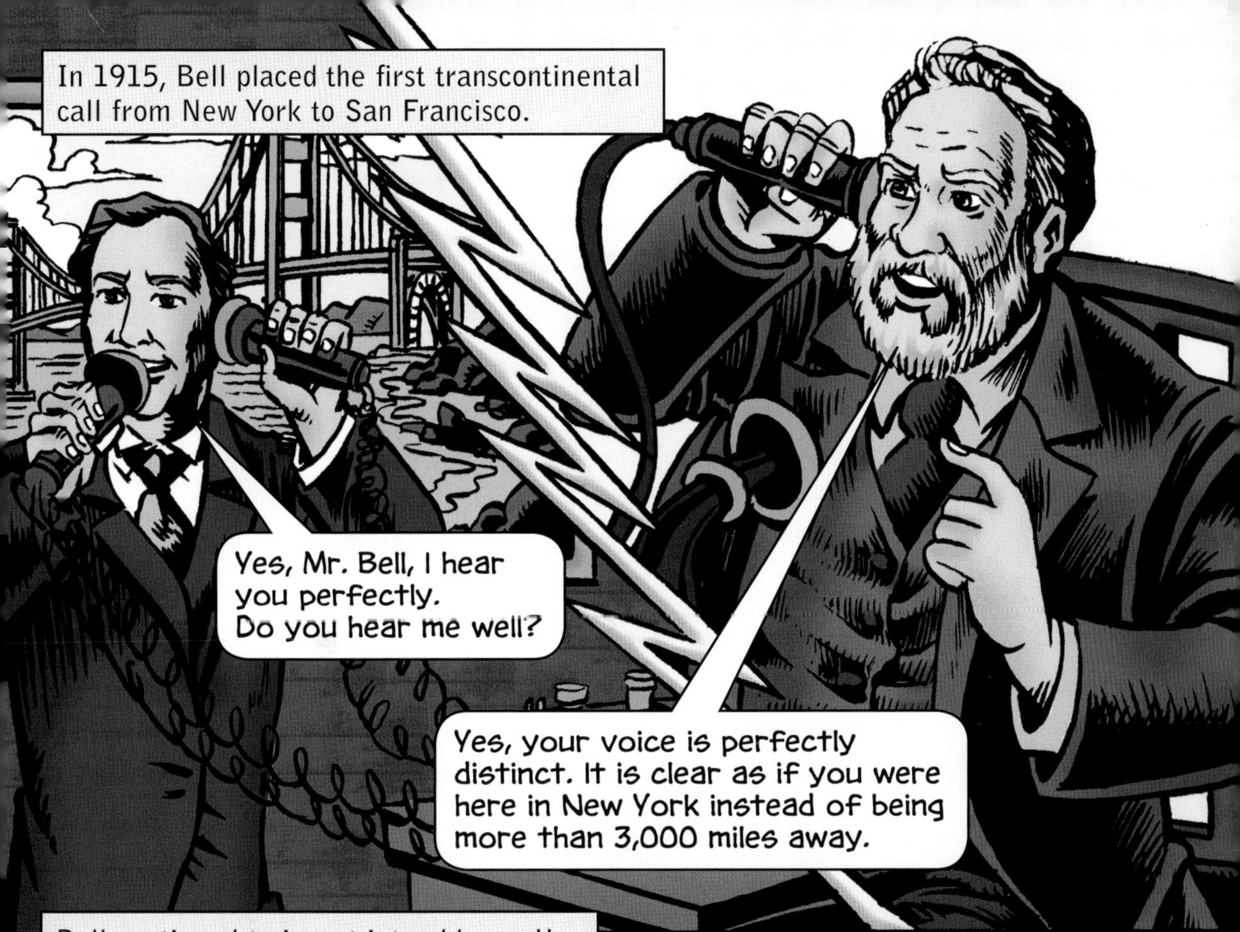
In 1915, Bell placed the first transcontinental call from New York to San Francisco.
Yes, Mr. Bell, I hear you perfectly. Do you hear me well?
Yes, your voice is perfectly distinct. It is clear as if you were here in New York instead of being more than 3,000 miles away.

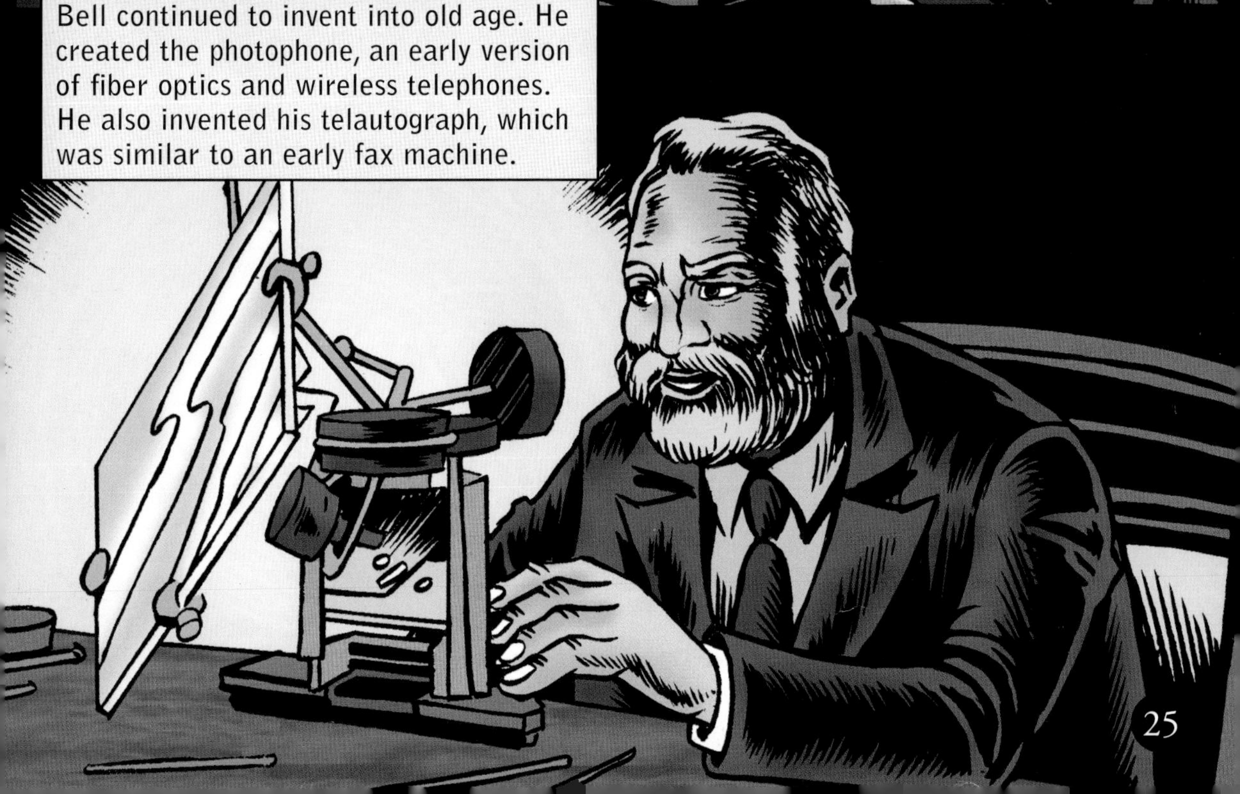
Bell continued to invent into old age. He created the photophone, an early version of fiber optics and wireless telephones. He also invented his telautograph, which was similar to an early fax machine.

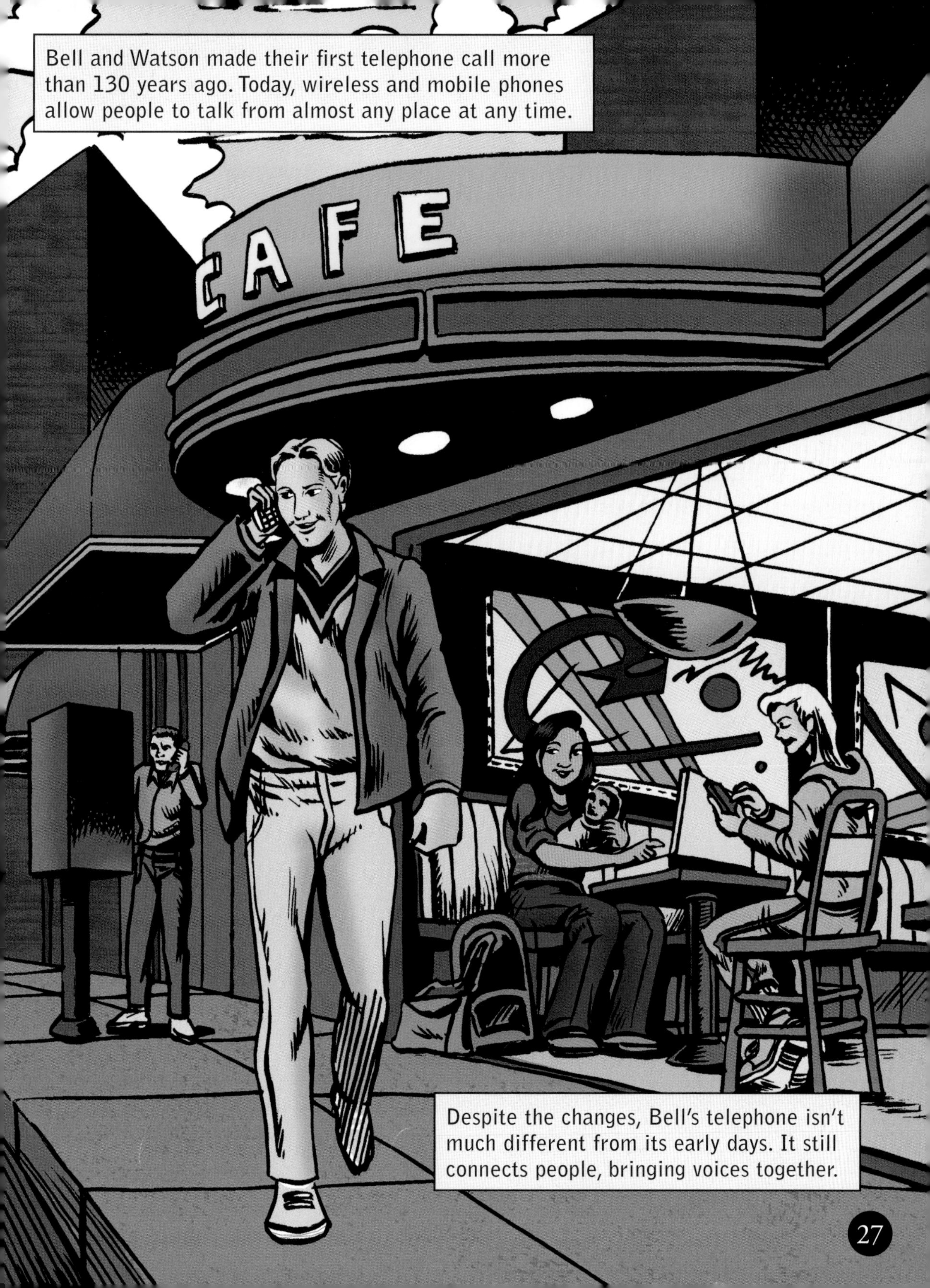
Bell and Watson made their first telephone call more than 130 years ago. Today, wireless and mobile phones allow people to talk from almost any place at any time.
CAFE
Despite the changes, Bell's telephone isn't much different from its early days. It still connects people, bringing voices together.

MORE ABOUT BELL AND THE
TELEPHONE

Alexander Graham Bell was born March 3, 1847, in Edinburgh, Scotland. He died at his home in Canada on August 2, 1922.

Bell believed his understanding of sound led him to create the first telephone. His father was an elocutionist, a person who teaches proper speech. He encouraged his sons to understand how the human voice works.

As teenagers, Bell and his brothers studied the human body and created a "speaking machine." They molded the mouth, tongue, throat, and lungs out of wax. When they forced air into the machine, they moved the mouth to form different words.

Bell worked as a teacher of elocution and music in his late teenage years. In his 20s, he worked as a teacher of the deaf, first in London, and then in the United States. Bell believed that deaf people should read lips and learn speech to communicate, instead of using sign language.

Bell married Mabel Hubbard, the daughter of Gardiner Greene Hubbard, in 1877. Mabel was deaf, and had been a student of Bell's.

The invention of the telephone has been debated since Bell received his first patent in 1876. In the 1850s, Italian immigrant Antonio Meucci began work on a talking telegraph. He filed paperwork for his idea in the U.S. patent office, but he never received a patent. Also, in the 1860s, a German schoolteacher named Philipp Reis invented a device that sent sounds electronically over wires. He tried to send voice over the wires, but there were problems with his device.

The decibel, the unit for measuring sound, is named after Bell.

In 1922, on the day of Alexander Graham Bell's funeral, all telephones in North America went silent for one minute to honor his life and his invention.

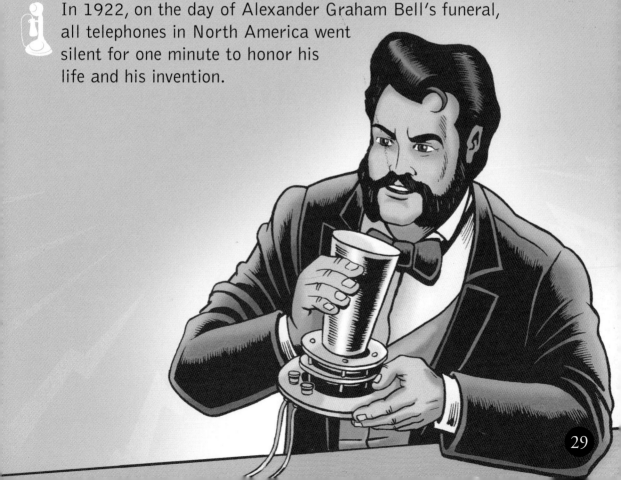

Glossary

harmonic (har-MON-ik)—a way to describe different sounds played at the same time

patent (PAT-uhnt)—a legal document that gives an inventor the right to make, use, or sell an invention for a set period of years

pitch (PICH)—the highness or lowness of a sound; vibrations change a sound's pitch.

satellite (SAT-uh-lite)—a spacecraft that circles the earth; satellites gather and send information.

transcontinental (transs-kon-tuh-NEN-tuhl)—extending or going across a continent

vibration (vye-BRA-shuhn)—a fast movement back and forth; vibrations in the throat are caused by air from the lungs.

Internet Sites

FactHound offers a safe, fun way to find Internet sites related to this book. All of the sites on FactHound have been researched by our staff.

Here's how:
1. Visit *www.facthound.com*
2. Choose your grade level.
3. Type in this book ID **0736864784** for age-appropriate sites. You may also browse subjects by clicking on letters, or by clicking on pictures and words.
4. Click on the **Fetch It** button.

FactHound will fetch the best sites for you!

READ MORE

Bankston, John. *Alexander Graham Bell and the Story of the Telephone.* Uncharted, Unexplored, and Unexplained. Hockessin, Del.: Mitchell Lane, 2005.

Durrett, Deanne. *Alexander Graham Bell.* Inventors and Creators. San Diego: KidHaven Press, 2003.

Jarnow, Jesse. *Telegraph and Telephone Networks: Groundbreaking Developments in American Communication.* America's Industrial Society in the 19th Century. New York: Rosen, 2004.

Nobleman, Marc Tyler. *The Telephone.* Great Inventions. Mankato, Minn.: Capstone Press, 2004.

BIBLIOGRAPHY

Alexander Graham Bell Family Papers at the
Library of Congress
http://memory.loc.gov/ammem/bellhtml/bellhome.html

Bruce, Robert V. *Bell: Alexander Graham Bell and the Conquest of Solitude.* Boston: Little, Brown, 1973.

Grosvenor, Edwin S., and Morgan Wesson. *Alexander Graham Bell: The Life and Times of the Man Who Invented the Telephone.* New York: Harry Abrams, 1997.

INDEX